ROUND
BY
ROUND

ROUND
BY
ROUND

In Search of Wisdom

FLORINE DOTSON EVANS

WESTBOW°
PRESS
A DIVISION OF THOMAS NELSON
& ZONDERVAN

WestBow Press books may be ordered through booksellers or by contacting:

WestBow Press
A Division of Thomas Nelson & Zondervan
1663 Liberty Drive
Bloomington, IN 47403
www.westbowpress.com
1 (866) 928-1240

Because of the dynamic nature of the Internet, any web addresses or
links contained in this book may have changed since publication and
may no longer be valid. The views expressed in this work are solely those
of the author and do not necessarily reflect the views of the publisher,
and the publisher hereby disclaims any responsibility for them.

Certain stock imagery © Thinkstock.
Any people depicted in stock imagery provided by Thinkstock are models,
and such images are being used for illustrative purposes only.

ISBN: 978-1-4908-3801-4 (e)
ISBN: 978-1-4908-3802-1 (sc)

Library of Congress Control Number: 2014909200

Printed in the United States of America.

WestBow Press rev. date: 8/27/2014

1. WE HAVE OUR WAY OF HAVING OUR WAY

2. YOUR PERSONAL POWER CANNOT BE TAKEN; YOU MUST AGREE TO SURRENDER IT.

3. THE MORE PEOPLE YOU KNOW, THE FEWER PEOPLE YOU REALLY KNOW.

4. WHAT YOU WERE TAUGHT IN KINDERGARTEN WILL TAKE A LIFETIME TO LEARN.

5. GUARD YOUR AFFECTION.

6. MAKE SOMEDAY, TODAY.

7. A GREAT LOSS CAN BE THE BREEDING GROUND FOR A GREAT VICTORY.

8. BECOME THE MASTER OF UNDERSTATEMENT.

9. WITH GOLDEN CORDS OF LOVING KINDNESS AND SILVER THREADS OF TENDER MERCIES, GOD CAN MEND THE BROKEN HEARTED.

10. GOD LETS TIME PASS AFTER A TRAGEDY BEFORE HE SENDS A BLESSING. HE GIVES US TIME TO HEAL, TIME TO FORGET THE PAIN SO WE CAN ENJOY THE BLESSING.

11. IF YOU'RE TOO BUSY TO HAVE A LIFE, MAYBE YOU'RE WATERING ARTIFICIAL FLOWERS.

12. WHEN A WOMAN WANTS TO BE EQUAL TO A MAN, SHE LIMITS HER POTENTIAL.

13. LIFE'S REGRETS JUST MAY BE THAT WE DID NOT FOLLOW OUR HUNCHES MORE OFTEN.

14. YOU CAN PUT A SQUARE PEG IN A ROUND HOLE IF THE SQUARE IS SMALL ENOUGH.

15. DON'T BE FRIGHTENED BY NUMBERS.

16. STUDY TO BE SILENT.

17. LET US TRAIN OURSELVES TO SPEAK THE WORD OF GOD.

18. YOU SHOULD BE AS KIND TO YOURSELF AS YOU ARE TO ANYONE ELSE.

19. BE YOUR OWN BEST FRIEND.

20. THE MORE PEOPLE TAKE ADVANTAGE OF YOU, THE MORE ADVANTAGE YOU HAVE LEFT.

21. TEARS WATER YOUR DREAMS.

22. IF AT FIRST YOU DON'T SUCCEED, HAVE A GOOD CRY AND START AGAIN.

23. NEVER UNDERESTIMATE THE POWER OF A SMILE.

24. EVERYTHING THAT I FEARED, HAPPENED.

25. ALL YOU CAN DO IS ALL YOU CAN DO.

26. WHEN YOU MAKE A MISTAKE, ADMIT IT.

27. THE MORE YOU HOARD, THE LESS YOU POSSESS.

28. GOD IS STILL ON THE THRONE AND PRAYER CHANGES THINGS.

29. DON'T HANG ON, HOLD ON.

30. CRYSTALLIZE YOUR THINKING.

31. SOMETIMES LOSING YOUR MIND IS THE BEST THING THAT CAN HAPPEN FOR YOU.

32. STAY IN THE MOMENT.

33. I AM NOT OFFENDED.

34. YOUR DAILY EXERCISE SHOULD BE BENDING YOUR KNEES IN PRAYER.

35. IF YOU CAN'T BE WRONG, YOU WILL NEVER BE RIGHT.

36. EVERY KNOCK IS A BOOST.

37. THERE IS NO REASON WHY YOU CAN'T BE HAPPY.

38. TAKE THE TIME TO WATCH A CANDLE BURN. YOU WILL BEGIN TO SEE THAT YOUR LIFE IS PRECIOUS.

39. LIVING IN THE PAST OR FEARING THE FUTURE PLACES YOUR LIFE ON HOLD.

40. ALL YOU WILL EVER NEED IS WITHIN YOU.

41. TAKE A "THANK YOU" WALK OFTEN.

42. YOU WILL ERR WHEN YOU RUN OUT OF FAITH.

43. PEOPLE WILL DISAPPOINT YOU. IT IS THE HUMAN CONDITION.

44. WHO ARE THE PEOPLE IN YOUR PEOPLE IN YOUR HEAD WHO TALK TO YOU EVERY DAY?

45. CHANGING YOUR MIND IS ONE OF YOUR OPTIONS.

46. IF YOUR SALES TEAM IS NOT HAVING FUN, THEY ARE NOT EARNING MONEY.

47. FOOD IS NOT MY FRIEND.

48. NOT TODAY.

49. WHEN YOU SUBMIT TO A TYRANT, YOU ARE SUPPORTING A TERRORIST.

50. SOMETIME YOU HAVE TO COME HOME.

51. IT IS ALREADY HAPPENING.

52. MISUSE OF KNOWLEDGE WILL LEAD TO GUILT, SHAME AND ULTIMATELY TO FEAR.

53. WHEN YOU BECOME TOTALLY ENLIGHTENED, YOU WILL LOVE UNCONDITIONALLY.

54. GO WITH THE FLOW.

55. GIVE TIME, TIME.

56. MAKE A LONG STORY SHORT.

57. THOUGHTS ARE THINGS.

58. IF YOU LOOK INTO THE MIRROR TOO LONG, THE MIRROR WILL START LYING TO YOU.

59. NEGOTIATE... NEGOTIATE.

60. YOU ARE THE SOLUTION.

61. SHARE YOUR VISIONS WITH FEW.

62. UNDERSTANDING WILL MAKE A PLACE FOR YOU.

63. GOD IS LOVE. HE LOVES JUSTICE AND ORDER.

64. THINK AS THOUGH NOTHING IS IMPOSSIBLE.

65. THE MOST BEAUTIFUL PEOPLE MAY NOT BE THE MOST ATTRACTIVE.

66. PLANT SOMETHING YOU WILL NOT SEE TO MATURITY.

67. I ENCOUNTERED A HEAVENLY BEING. HE DID NOT HAVE WINGS.

68. UP ABOVE YOUR HEAD ARE BLESSINGS WAITING TO BE CLAIMED.

69. WISDOM IS THE PRINCIPLE THING.

70. SEND FAITH TO ANSWER ANY QUESTIONS FEAR MAY BRING.

71. YOU MAY BE IN
A GREAT STRUGGLE,
BUT DON'T LOSE HOPE.
YOU WILL PREVAIL…
ROUND BY ROUND.